THE POWER OF
INFLUENCE

by
John C. Maxwell

RIVER
OAK
PUBLISHING

The Power of Influence
ISBN 1-58919-410-1
Copyright © 2001 by John C. Maxwell

Published by RiverOak Publishing
P.O. Box 700143
Tulsa, Oklahoma 74170-0143

Introduction

Millionaire industrialist John D. Rockefeller once said that he was willing to pay more for this ability than any other under the sun. President Theodore Roosevelt said it was the most important ingredient in the formula of success. The quality? Influence—our ability to deal with people and build positive relationships with them. More than anything else in life, relationships make or break us.

That's why it's important to keep learning about relationships and how to influence people for good. This book is designed as a short course on relationship building through positive influence. May these timeless quotes and insights from men and women who understand people help you discover and cultivate the power of influence.

—John C. Maxwell

The Ten Commandments
of Human Relations:

1. Speak to people.

2. Smile at people.

3. Call people by name.

4. Be friendly and helpful.

5. Be cordial.

6. Have a genuine interest in people.

7. Be generous with praise.

8. Be considerate of the feelings of others.

9. Be thoughtful of the opinions of others.

10. Be alert to give service.

If you're going to play together as
a team, you've got to care for one
another. You've got to love each other.

— Vince Lombardi

The Law of Relationship says that
every person is merely four people
away from any other human on earth.

I don't know the key to success,
but the key to failure is
trying to please everybody.

—Bill Cosby

No matter how much work
you can do, no matter how
engaging your personality may be,
you will not advance far in business
if you cannot work through others.

—John Craig

You can't be any closer to God than you are to the person you love least.

You can't make the other fellow feel important in your presence if you secretly feel that he is a nobody.

—Les Giblin

It is very easy to forgive others
their mistakes; it takes more grit
and gumption to forgive them
for having witnessed your own.

—Jessamyn West

People aren't sales resistant—
they are salespeople resistant.

—Mark Hebenstreit

Numbers don't mean anything . . .
because it's people that count.

—Will Rogers

$$R + R - R = R + R$$
(Rules and Regulations minus Relationships
equals Resentment and Rebellion)

A drop of honey catches
more flies than a gallon of gall.

—Abraham Lincoln

Friendship flourishes at
the fountain of forgiveness.

—William A. Ward

If someone hurts you,
first try to figure out whether
that hurt was intentional or not.
Not every hurt is an attack.

Getting people to like you is merely
the other side of liking them.

———————————

Ninety percent of the friction
of daily life is caused by
the wrong tone of voice.

It is well to remember that the
entire population of the universe
with one trifling exception
is composed of others.

J.A. Holmes

If you want to get along with people,
pretend you never knew
whatever they tell you.

―――――――――

Each relationship nurtures a
strength or weakness within you.

Few things will pay you bigger
dividends than the time and trouble
you take to understand people.
Almost nothing will add more to
your stature as an executive
and a person. Nothing will
give you greater satisfaction or
bring you more happiness.

—Kienzle and Dare

Do to others as you
would have them do to you.

—Jesus (Luke 6:31 NIV)

_____

A great man shows his greatness
by the way he treats little men.

—Thomas Carlyle

If you want to lose friends quickly,
start bragging about yourself; if
you want to make and keep friends,
start bragging about others.

I will speak ill of no man and speak
all the good I know of everybody.

—Benjamin Franklin

The true test of being
comfortable with someone else
is the ability to share silence.

—Frank Tyger

The man who goes alone can
start the day. But he who
travels with another must
wait until the other is ready.

—Henry David Thoreau

Relationships are
not formed but forged.

_____

Anyone who loves his opinions
more than he does his brethren
will defend his opinions
and destroy his brethren.

Let another man praise thee, and
not thine own mouth; a stranger,
and not thine own lips.

—Proverbs 27:2

You cannot shake hands
with a clenched fist.

—Indira Gandhi

———————————

To handle yourself, use your head.
To handle others, use your heart.

—John C. Maxwell

Ninety percent of the art of
living consists of getting along
with people you cannot stand.

—Samuel Goldwyn

Instead of putting others in their place,
put yourself in their place.

———————————————

Every man is entitled to be
valued by his best moments.

—Ralph Waldo Emerson

Natural talent, intelligence, a wonderful
education—none of these guarantees
success. Something else is needed:
the sensitivity to understand
what other people want and the
willingness to give it to them.

—John Luther

One man working with you is worth
a dozen men working for you.

—Herman M. Koelliker

People don't care how much
you know until they know
how much you care.

—John C. Maxwell

If you would win a man to
your cause, first convince him
that you are his sincere friend.

—Abraham Lincoln

The most important single ingredient
in the formula of success is knowing
how to get along with people.

—Theodore Roosevelt

I will pay more for the ability
to deal with people than for
any other ability under the sun.

—John D. Rockefeller

There is a rule in sailing that
the more maneuverable ship
should give way to the less
maneuverable craft. I think this is
sometimes a good rule to follow
in human relationships as well.

—Dr. Joyce Brothers

If you are suffering from a
bad man's injustice, forgive him
lest there be two bad men.

—Augustine

Seek to be a plow rather than a
bulldozer. The plow cultivates the soil,
making it a good place for seed to grow.
The bulldozer scrapes the earth and
pushes every obstacle out of the way.

A Short Course in Human Relations . . .

The Six Most Important Words:
"I admit I made a mistake."

The Five Most Important Words:
"You did a good job."

The Four Most Important Words:
"What is your opinion?"

The Three Most Important Words:
"If you please."

The Two Most Important Words:
"Thank you."

The Most Important Word: "We."

The Least Important Word: "I."

Don't use your people to
build a great work; use your
work to build a great people.

—Jack Hyles

———————————

There is no more noble
occupation in the world than to
assist another human being—
to help someone succeed.

—Alan Loy McGinnis

Practice the 101 percent principle:
Find the 1 thing you agree on
with another person, and then give
100 percent of your encouragement.

—John C. Maxwell

Assets make things possible.
People make things happen.

_____

You can tell more about a person
by what he says about others than
you can by what others say about him.

It is one of the most beautiful
compensations of this life that
no man can sincerely try to help
another without helping himself.

—Ralph Waldo Emerson

In getting along with others,
98 percent depends on
our behavior with others.

———————————

Marriage is the only union that
can't be organized. Both sides
think they're management.

—*Funny Funny World*

If you would have a happy life,
remember two things: In matters of
principle, stand like a rock; in matters
of taste, swim with the current.

—Thomas Jefferson

We never know the love
of our parents for us till
we have become parents.

—Henry Ward Beecher

My most brilliant achievement
was my ability to be able to
persuade my wife to marry me.

—Winston Churchill

Two are better than one, because they
have a good return for their work:
If one falls down, his friend can help
him up. But pity the man who falls
and has no one to help him up!

—Ecclesiastes 4:9-10 NIV

Even marriages made in heaven need down-to-earth maintenance work.

—Lloyd Byers

_____

It is not marriage that fails, it is people that fail. All that marriage does is to show people up.

—Harry Emerson Fosdick

To keep the fire burning brightly, keep the two logs together, near enough to keep each other warm, and far enough apart—about a finger's breadth—for breathing room. Good fire, good marriage—same rule.

—Marnie Reed Crowell

God is the only third party in a
marriage that can make it work.

_____

Faith makes all things possible.
Love makes all things easy.
Hope makes all things work.

Before a marriage, a man
will lie awake all night thinking
about something you said;
after marriage, he'll fall asleep
before you finish saying it.

—Helen Rowland

The key to a perfect marriage
is not expecting perfection.

Marriage is an empty box.
It remains empty unless you
put in more than you take out.

Love at first sight is nothing special.
It's when two people have been
looking at each other for years
that it becomes a miracle.

—Sam Levinson

Courtship brings out the best.
Marriage bring out the rest.

—Cullen Hightower

———————————

Love will find a way.
Indifference will find an excuse.

There are two great motivators in life.
One is fear. The other is love.
You can lead an organization
by fear, but if you do, you will
ensure that people won't perform
up to their real capabilities.

—Jan Carlson

We may not choose whom we
will love if we claim to be Christians.

———————————————

A person needs to be loved
the most when he deserves
to be loved the least.

The biggest disease today is
not leprosy or tuberculosis,
but rather the feeling of
being unwanted, uncared for,
and deserted by everybody.

—Mother Teresa

Truth without love is brutality.
Love without truth is hypocrisy.

The love of our neighbor
is the only door out of
the dungeon of self.

—George MacDonald

Genuine love is a fragile flower.
It must be maintained and protected
if it is to survive. Love can perish . . .
when there is no time for romantic
activity . . . when a man and his wife
forget how to talk to each other.

—James Dobson

Faults are thick where love is thin.

The law of love always supersedes
the law of personal liberty.

You will find as you look back
upon your life that the moments
when you have really lived are
the moments when you have
done things in the spirit of love.

—Henry Drummond

If you want to make your mother
happy, talk to her. If you want
to make your father happy, listen.

Human beings are the only
creatures on earth that allow
their children to come back home.

—Bill Cosby

How far you go in life depends on
your being tender with the young,
compassionate with the aged,
sympathetic with the striving, and
tolerant of the weak and the strong.
Because some day in life
you will have been all of these.

—George Washington Carver

A man should choose for his wife
the woman he would choose as
his best friend, were she a man.

———————————

There is no lonelier person
than the one who lives with
a spouse with whom he or
she cannot communicate.

—Margaret Mead

When I'm getting ready to reason
with a man, I spend one-third of
my time thinking about myself
and what I am going to say—
and two-thirds thinking about
him and what he is going to say.

—Abraham Lincoln

People are lonely because they
build walls instead of bridges.

—Joseph F. Newton

_____

It's when you rub elbows
with a man that you find out
what he has up his sleeve.

To keep your marriage brimming

With love in the loving cup,

When you're wrong, admit it.

When you're right, shut up.

—Ogden Nash

Successful marriage is always a
triangle: a man, a woman, and God.

—Cecil Myers

Train up a child in the way
he should go—and walk there
yourself once in a while.

—Josh Billings

Parents are prone to give their children
everything except the one thing
they need most. That is time.

—Emma K. Hulburt

Never try to make your son or
daughter another you; one is enough!

—Arnold Glasow

The best gift a father can
give to his son is the gift
of himself—his time.

—C. Neil Strait

The most important thing that
parents can teach their children is
how to get along without them.

−Frank A. Clark

By the time we realize our parents
may have been right, we usually have
children who think we are wrong.

_____

If there is anything better
than being loved, it's loving.

There is no more lovely, friendly, and
charming relationship, communion,
or company than a good marriage.

—Martin Luther

God chooses our relatives;
we choose our friends.

_____

Never be yoked to one
who refuses the yoke of Christ.

The formula for achieving a
successful relationship is simple:
You should treat all disasters as if
they were trivialities, but never treat
a triviality as if it were a disaster.

—Quentin Crisp

Most communication problems
can be solved with proximity.

_____

Man and melons are hard to know.

—Benjamin Franklin

A gossip is one who talks to you
about others; a bore is one who
talks to you about himself; and a
brilliant conversationalist is one
who talks to you about yourself.

—Lisa Kirk

A person whose ship has
come in usually finds most
of his relatives at the dock.

––––––––––––––––––

The harder you work at a relationship,
the harder it is to surrender.

The opinions which we hold
of one another, our relationships
with friends and kinsfolk are
in no sense permanent, save in
appearance, but are as eternally
fluid as the sea itself.

—Marcel Proust

A man is known by the
company he organizes.

—Ambrose Pierce

———————————

A wise man associating with
the vicious becomes an idiot;
a dog traveling with good men
becomes a rational being.

—Arabic Proverb

You will acquire the vices and
virtues of your closest associates.
The fragrance of their lives
will pervade your life.

—John C. Maxwell

Tell me thy company, and
I'll tell thee what thou art.

—Cervantes

_____

Every man is like the company
he is wont to keep.

—Euripides

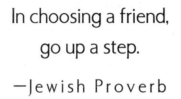

In choosing a friend,

go up a step.

—Jewish Proverb

A wise man may look ridiculous
in the company of fools.

—Thomas Fuller

_____

He that lies down with dogs
shall rise up with flies.

—Latin Proverb

It is better to weep with wise men
than to laugh with fools.

—Spanish Proverb

Familiarity breeds
contempt—and children.

—Mark Twain

_____

Satan's friendship reaches
to the prison door.

—Turkish Proverb

We cannot forgive another
for not being ourselves.

—Ralph Waldo Emerson

None knows the weight
of another's burden.

—Thomas Fuller

Just as much as we see in
others we have in ourselves.

—William Hazlitt

Most often it happens that one
attributes to others only the feelings
of which one is capable oneself.

—André Gide

The longer we live, the more
we find we are like other persons.

—Oliver Wendell Holmes

_____

Hurting people hurt people.

—John C. Maxwell

No man is much pleased
with a companion who does
not increase, in some respect,
his fondness of himself.

—Samuel Johnson

Love or perish.

_____

One learns peoples
through the heart, not
the eyes or the intellect.

—Mark Twain

Don't drown the man who taught
you to swim. If you learned your
trade or profession from the man,
do not set up in opposition to him.

—C. H. Spurgeon

It is a wise father that
knows his own child.

—Shakespeare

What the mother sings
to the cradle goes all the
way down to the coffin.

—Henry Ward Beecher

It is the atmosphere created
primarily by the mother that
makes a home worthwhile.

—J. R. Bookhoff

A father is a banker
provided by nature.

—French Proverb

You don't have to deserve
your mother's love. You have
to deserve you father's.
He's more particular.

—Robert Frost

Where parents do too much
for their children, the children
will not do much for themselves.

—Elbert Hubbard

An angry father is most
cruel toward himself.

—Publilius Syrus

_____

Every beetle is a gazelle
in the eyes of its mother.

—Moorish Proverb

Romance fails us and so do
friendships, but the relationship of
parent and child, less noisy than
all others, remains indelible and
indestructible, the strongest
relationship on earth.

—Theodore Reik

There is scarcity of friendship,
but not of friends.

—Thomas Fuller

Acquaintance, n. A person
whom we know well enough
to borrow from, but not
well enough to lend to.

—Ambrose Pierce

A companion loves some
agreeable qualities which a man
may possess, but a friend
loves the man himself.

—James Boswell

It is by forgiving that one is forgiven.

—Mother Teresa

A man should keep his
friendship in constant repair.

—Samuel Johnson

Forsake not an old friend, for a
new one does not compare with him.

—The Apocrypha

Between friends there
is no need of justice.

—Aristotle

_____

Of all the things granted
by wisdom, none is greater
or better than friendship.

—Pietro Aretino

Friendship is a strong habitual
inclination in two persons
to promote the good and
happiness of one another.

—Eustace Budgell

Wishing to be friends is
quick work, but friendship
is a slow-ripening fruit.

—Aristotle

Faithful are the wounds of
a friend; but the kisses of
an enemy are deceitful.

—Proverbs 27:6

The firmest friendships have been
formed in mutual adversity,
as iron is most strongly
united by the fiercest flame.

—Charles Caleb Colton

True friendship is like sound health;
the value of it is seldom
known until it be lost.

—Charles Caleb Colton

_____

Friendship makes prosperity more
brilliant and lightens adversity
by dividing and sharing it.

—Cicero

The friendships which last are those wherein each friend respects the other's dignity to the point of not really wanting anything from him.

—Cyril Connolly

The real friendships among men
are so rare that when they
occur they are famous.

—Clarence Day

It is one of the blessings of
old friends that you can
afford to be stupid with them.

—Ralph Waldo Emerson

Real friendship is shown in
times of trouble; prosperity
is full of friends.

—Euripides

The only way to have
a friend is to be one.

—Ralph Waldo Emerson

_____

One loyal friend is worth
ten thousand relatives.

—Euripides

A friend is a person with whom
I may be sincere. Before him,
I may think aloud.

—Ralph Waldo Emerson

A good friend is my nearest relation.

—Thomas Fuller

_____

Friendship multiplies the good
of life and divides the evil.

—Baltasar Gracián

A friend may well be reckoned
the masterpiece of nature.

—Ralph Waldo Emerson

A sympathetic friend can be
quite as dear as a brother.

—Homer

_____

Your friend is a man who knows
all about you, and still likes you.

—Elbert Hubbard

Love is rarer than genius itself.
And friendship is rarer still.

—Charles Péguy

A true friend is the
greatest of all blessings.

—François La Rochefoucauld

———————————

Hold a true friend
with both your hands.

—Nigerian Proverb

The proper office of a friend is
to side with you when you are in
the wrong. Nearly anybody will side
with you when you are in the right.

—Mark Twain

Friendship either finds
or makes equals.

—Publilius Syrus

A man cannot be said to
succeed in this life who
does not satisfy one friend.

—Henry David Thoreau

You cannot be friends upon
any other terms than upon
the terms of equality.

— Woodrow Wilson

Whoso findeth a wife
findeth a good thing.

—Proverbs 18:22

_____

Can two walk together,
except they be agreed?

—Amos 3:3

Marriage is the perfection
which love aimed at,
ignorant of what is sought.

—Ralph Waldo Emerson

A rare spoil for a man is
the winning of a good wife.

—Euripides

_____

Only a person who has
faith in himself is able
to be faithful to others.

—Erich Fromm

There is nothing nobler or more
admirable than when two people
who see eye to eye keep house
as man and wife, confounding their
enemies and delighting their friends.

—Homer

A man's best fortune,
or his worst, is his wife.

—Thomas Fuller

The love we have in our youth
is superficial compared to the love
that an old man has for his old wife.

—Will Durant
(On his 90th birthday)

A man should be taller, older,
heavier, uglier, and hoarser
than his wife.

—Edgar Watson Howe

Man's best asset is
a sympathetic wife.

—Euripides

_____

An ideal wife is any woman
who has an ideal husband.

—Booth Tarkington

There are six requisites in every
happy marriage. The first is Faith and
the remaining five are Confidence.

—Elbert Hubbard

Every mother is like Moses. She
does not enter the promised land.
She prepares a world she will not see.

—Pope Paul VI

Back of every achievement
is a proud wife and a
surprised mother-in-law.

—Brooks Hays

No man knows what the wife
of his bosom is until he has
gone with her through the
fiery trials of this world.

—Washington Irving

There is more pleasure in
loving than in being beloved.

—Thomas Fuller

We should measure affection,
not like youngsters by the ardor
of our passion, but by its
strength and constancy.

—Cicero

A successful marriage requires
falling in love many times,
always with the same person.

—Mignon McLaughlin

Give every man thine ear,
but few thy voice.

—Shakespeare

Most Americans don't,
in any vital sense, get together;
they only do things together.

—Louis Kronberger

Never speak of yourself to others;
make them talk about themselves
instead: therein lies the whole art
of pleasing. Everyone knows
it and everyone forgets it.

—Edmond and Jules de Goncourt

A single arrow is easily broken,
but not ten in a bundle.

—Japanese Proverb

Behold, how good and how
pleasant it is for brethren
to dwell together in unity!

—Psalm 133:1

The holy passion of friendship is
so sweet and steady and loyal
and enduring in nature that it
will last through a whole lifetime,
if not asked to lend money.

—Mark Twain

Whoso loves believes
the impossible.

—Elizabeth Barrett Browning

Many waters cannot quench love,
neither can the floods drown it.

—Song of Solomon 8:7

Love means giving one's
self to another person fully,
not just physically. When two
people really love each other, this
helps them to stay alive and grow.
One must really be loved to grow.

—Nancy Reagan

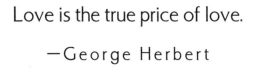

Love is the true price of love.

—George Herbert

_____

The course of love
never did run smooth.

—Shakespeare

Greater love hath no man
than this, that a man lay down
his life for his friends.

—Jesus (John 15:13)

If you've never been hated by
your child, you've never been a parent.

—Bette Davis

I have found the best way
to give advice to your children
is to find out what they want
and then advise them to do it.

—Harry S Truman

I talk and talk, and I haven't taught people in fifty years what my father taught by example in one week.

—Mario Cuomo

The most important thing
a father can do for his children
is to love their mother.

—Theodore M. Hesburgh

Every generation revolts
against its fathers and makes
friends with its grandfathers.

—Lewis Mumford

Build me a son, O Lord,
who will be strong enough to
know when he is weak, and brave
enough to face himself when he is
afraid, one who will be proud and
unbending in honest defeat, and
humble and gentle in victory.

—Prayer of Douglas MacArthur

Other things may change us,
but we start and end with family.

—Anthony Brandt

_____

You don't choose your family.
They are God's gift to you,
as you are to them.

—Desmond Tutu

In the next year or so, my
signature will appear on $60 billion
of United States currency.
More important to me, however,
is the signature that appears on
my life—the strong, proud,
assertive handwriting of
a loving father and mother.

—Katherine D. Ortega,
U.S. Treasurer

We need a better family life to
make us better servants of the people.

—Jimmy Carter

Spoil your husband, but don't spoil
your children—that's my philosophy.

—Louise Sevier Giddings Currey,
1961 *New York Post* Mother of the Year

President Johnson and I have a
lot in common. We were both born
in small towns ... and we're both
fortunate in the fact that we think
we married above ourselves.

—Richard M. Nixon

Success in marriage does not come
merely through finding the right mate,
but through being the right mate.

—Barnett Brickner

Marriage is not just spiritual
communion and passionate embraces;
marriage is also three meals a day and
remembering to carry out the trash.

—Dr. Joyce Brothers

The family is one of
nature's masterpieces.

—George Santayana

Bringing up a family
should be an adventure.

—Milton R. Sapirstein

Our children are not going
to be just "our children"—
they are going to be other
people's husbands and wives and
the parents of our grandchildren.

—Mary S. Calderone

A boy becomes an adult three
years before his parents think
he does and about two years
after he thinks he does.

—Lewis B. Hershey

Parenthood remains the greatest
single preserve of the amateur.

—Alvin Toffler

_____

More than in any other human
relationship, overwhelmingly more,
motherhood means being instantly
interruptible, responsive, responsible.

—Tille Olsen

Friendship with oneself is
all-important, because without
it one cannot be friends
with anyone else in the world.

—Eleanor Roosevelt

Once you get people laughing,
they're listening and you can
tell them almost anything.

—Herbert Gardner

_____

A person reveals his character
by nothing so clearly
as the joke he resents.

—G.C. Lichtenberg

Among those whom I like, I can
find no common denominator,
but among those whom I love,
I can; all of them make me laugh.

— W.H. Auden

As iron sharpens iron, so
one man sharpens another.

—Proverbs 27:17 NIV

If a man does not make new
acquaintances as he advances
through life, he will soon
find himself left alone.

—Samuel Johnson

When the character of a man is
not clear to you, look at his friends.

—Japanese Proverb

Be wiser than other people,
if you can, but do not tell them so.

—Lord Chesterfield

———————————

Sometimes it's worse
to win a fight than to lose.

—Billie Holiday

A friend can tell you things
you don't want to tell yourself.

—Frances Ward Weller

The richer your friends,
the more they will cost you.

—Elisabeth Marbury

_____

If you want to grow up, go up.
Associate with people whose
achievements exceed your own
and model the growth you desire.

—John C. Maxwell

No man is an island entire
of itself; every man is a part of
the continent, a part of the main.

—John Donne

About the Author

John Maxwell is one of the world's most respected authorities on leadership and personal effectiveness. He has written more than twenty books, including the *New York Times* best seller *The 21 Irrefutable Laws of Leadership*, which has sold more than half a million copies. In addition to his writing career, he is a popular speaker, inspiring more than 250,000 people annually at appearances nationwide.

Dr. Maxwell's advice is based on his thirty-plus years of experience as a pastoral and organizational leader. He is founder of the INJOY Group, an organization that helps people maximize their personal and leadership potential. And he has served as a senior pastor for churches in California, Ohio, and Indiana.

The father of two grown children, Dr. Maxwell lives in Atlanta, Georgia, with Margaret, his wife of more than twenty-five years.

Additional copies of this book and other titles by John C. Maxwell are available from your local bookstore.

The Power of Leadership
The Power of Attitude
The Power of Thinking Big

RIVER OAK
PUBLISHING